Creative Homework Tasks

Activities to Challenge and Inspire 7–9 Year Olds

Giles Hughes

Brilliant
PUBLICATIONS

Publishers Information

Other books of interest:
Creative Homework Tasks: Activities to Challenge and Inspire 9–11 Year Olds
Brilliant Activities for Gifted and Talented Children
Brilliant Activities for Stretching Gifted and Talented Children
Thinking Strategies for 5–7 Year Olds
Thinking Strategies for 7–9 Year Olds
Thinking Strategies for 9–11 Year Olds

Published by Brilliant Publications
Unit 10,
Sparrow Hall Farm,
Edlesborough,
Dunstable,
Bedfordshire,
LU6 2ES

Website: www.brilliantpublications.co.uk
General information enquiries:
Tel: 01525 222292

The name 'Brilliant Publications'
and the logo are registered trade marks.

Written by Giles Hughes
Illustrated by Frank Endersby
Cover illustration by Frank Endersby
Printed in the UK

© 2010 Giles Hughes (text); Brilliant Publications (design and layout)
Printed ISBN: 978-1-905780-55-6
Ebook ISBN: 978-0-85747-001-0
First published 2010
10 9 8 7 6 5 4 3 2 1

Contents

Introduction

It's a Friday afternoon and in schools across the country audible groans of disappointment filter from each classroom as homework assignments are given out.

On Sunday evenings tensions rise in family homes as parents and their children begin negotiations, threats, sulks and bribery over uncompleted homework.

Back at school on the following Monday mornings, teachers begin to chase up the late and missing homework tasks. Once again, the nation's dogs have developed a taste for paper, homework booklets have mysteriously vanished into thin air and thousands of homework sheets have been left on the back seats of cars and buses.

Does this sound all too familiar? Teachers, pupils and parents seem to accept these rituals as an unavoidable part of school life.

In writing these *Creative Homework Tasks* I decided to try to change this pattern of behaviour. As a busy teacher, and parent, I felt homework was an extra source of stress I could do without and set out to find a solution that would suit everyone.

My first undertaking was to look at a variety of homework schemes and assess the quality and variety of homework assignments. The vast majority of homework tasks were numeracy and literacy based, the sheets themselves tended to look similar, generally being formal in layout and lacking pictures, diagrams and illustrations.

It was obvious that these tasks were completely inappropriate for the largest group of non-participants, most of whom were boys. I invited groups of children to carry out a 'preferred learning style' questionnaire. The results indicated that the majority of children who were reluctant to carry out homework tasks were kinaesthetic learners and visual learners.

When asked to list things that they were interested in outside of school and their favourite school lessons, football, art, science fiction, dinosaurs, sport, computer games and crafts all figured highly on their lists!

Knowing what the children were interested in and how they preferred to learn gave me something tangible to go on – my job was to now go out and plan a series of new homework tasks that would appeal directly to them.

The first creative homework task I came up with was one where they had to invent their own 'James Bond' style watch (*Escape* pages 34–35). The watch design had to incorporate three gadgets which their 'hero' uses to defeat or escape from an enemy.

Children love secrets and an element of mystery, so in order to attract their interest I staged this first task. On Monday morning I sat with my back to the class working at my desk before calling the register, apparently engrossed in what I was doing. Within moments I was surrounded by a group of inquisitive children eager to see what I was up to. Quickly I covered my work, giving just enough time for them to see I had been busy drawing something. Despite constant pestering I refused to tell them what my sketch was of. I continued this charade during the day, making sure that news and occasional glimpses of my 'Design a Gadget Watch' homework sheet slowly filtered around the class. The design of the sheet was highly visual, keeping text down to a minimum.

On Friday I introduced the task to the children, proudly showing my watch design and explaining its functions. To my amazement two of the boys called out, 'we've already done ours, we sneaked in at playtime and saw it on your desk!' These two individuals, who hadn't managed a single piece of homework between them all year, now produced finished watch designs and stories from their bags! That week every child in the class completed their homework on time and I realized I was onto a winner.

Over the next year, the number of children participating in homework rose as they worked their way through the new creative tasks. In addition, feedback from parents was extremely positive, many noticing a positive change in their children's attitude towards homework. In many cases it seemed the format and content of these new homework tasks was putting an end to the confrontation, arguments and bribery the parents previously resorted to in order to ensure homework was done.

Indeed, one boy's homework had improved beyond recognition. His handwriting, spelling, grammar, design skills and drawing were a revelation. Alas, it was too good to be true, the new tasks had proved to be a temptation for his father who had completed them himself! The boy ended up taking two copies home so that they could work together, even then his father insisted on handing his homework in too!

Once a new ethos was established in class I started to introduce tasks that appealed to a wider audience. My first tasks were developed with underachieving, kinaesthetic boys in mind. I gambled that if I kept the tasks visually stimulating and creative in nature these children would still retain their new-found enthusiasm. It was also important to start introducing a wider range of curriculum areas, particularly numeracy and literacy while doing away with lists of sums, lengthy explanations and mountains of text. Devising tasks that get children to think creatively, or giving traditional tasks a creative twist, is the key.

The tasks you will find in this book have been trialled in a number of schools and are the culmination of many months of research, feedback and editing. They have been designed so that they can be given out with little or no input from the teacher if need be. In my experience a little enthusiasm from the teacher goes a long way. There are extensive teacher notes for each task – giving examples of extension activities, relevant websites, fun ways of accessing the tasks and solutions to the problems!

There are some great ideas in the book that all children will love – many seem too good to waste on homework! Why not start them off at school or dip into the teacher's notes to find an extension exercise to do at home?

Above all, enjoy the tasks – homework no longer needs to be a grind!

Duster Slippers for Cats!

The task for the children is to write and illustrate an advert that will persuade people to buy 'Duster Slippers' for their cats. The children will need to exaggerate any positive features they can think of for this invention.

Encourage the children to use the persuasive strategies listed on the sheet. Using them will make their advert more effective.

For example, use questions such as:

■   Is dust a problem in your house?

■   Could you do with more help with the housework?

■   Is it about time that your pet started to pull its weight?

Or use instructions or promise and exaggerations such as:

■   You need Duster Slippers for Cats!

■   Try Duster Slippers for Cats today! (instruction)

■   This amazing new product will put an end to all your dusting worries!

■   See what a difference they make – satisfaction guaranteed (Promise)

You could give customers a warning/important advice, with:

■   Don't miss out on the opportunity of a lifetime (advice/warning)

And finally, use expert opinion to endorse the product:

■   'I bought *Duster Slippers for Cats* for our cats Tiddles and Diddles, and Victoria hasn't lifted a duster since.' (David Beckham – International footballer).

Duster Slippers for Cats!

Is this a useless invention?

Do you think that these slippers would help with the housework?

Can you work out why they are such a useless invention?

Your task is to write and illustrate an advert that will persuade people to buy 'Duster Slippers' for their cats.

Try using the following strategies to make your advert more persuasive:

Exaggerate:
'This new product will change your life.'

Promise:
'I give my word that …'
'Guaranteed to … '

Instruct:
'Buy a set today!'

Question:
'Do you want a filthy, dusty house?'

Invitation:
'Try using Duster Slippers on your moggy.'

Advice/Warning:
'Without Duster Slippers your house will be covered in dust!'

Expert Opinion:
'9 out of 10 vets recommend this product.'

© Giles Hughes and Brilliant Publications
Creative Homework Tasks, 7–9 Year Olds

Word Squares

Explain what a word square is and tell the children that their task is to complete the following and then to make some of their own to test their parents and friends.

The 3x3 grids are quite simple to complete, there are many different solutions to the examples on the task sheet. Here are some possible solutions.

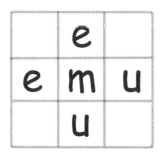

	a	
a	r	e
	e	

t	a	p
a	r	e
p	e	n

b	a	t
a	r	e
t	e	n

c	a	t
a	r	e
t	e	a

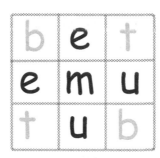

	e	
e	m	u
	u	

b	e	t
e	m	u
t	u	b

p	e	n
e	m	u
n	u	t

b	e	g
e	m	u
g	u	n

	a	
a	c	e
	e	

p	a	t
a	c	e
t	e	n

m	a	n
a	c	e
n	e	t

r	a	g
a	c	e
g	e	t

It is worth pointing out that the central word through the 3x3 grid is always vowel/consonant/vowel. This will help when the children design their own 3x3 word squares.

4x4 word squares are more complicated. Here are possible solutions for the examples on the homework task sheet.

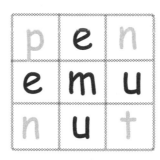

s	n	o	w
n		n	
o	n	c	e
w		e	

s	n	o	w
n	i	n	e
o	n	c	e
w	e	e	k

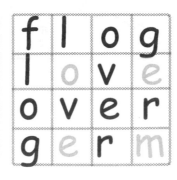

f	l	o	g
l		v	
o	v	e	r
g		r	

f	l	o	g
l	o	v	e
o	v	e	r
g	e	r	m

d	a	f	t
a	b	l	e
f	l		
t	e		

d	a	f	t
a	b	l	e
f	l	e	a
t	e	a	m

8

© Giles Hughes and Brilliant Publications
Creative Homework Tasks, 7–9 Year Olds

Word Squares

Can you fill a square with a set of words that both go across and down at the same time?

Here are two examples using three letter words in a 3 x 3 grid.

b	i	n
i	c	e
n	e	w

m	a	t
a	t	e
t	e	n

Can you find a way to complete these three grids below?

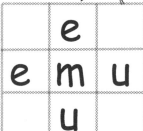

	a	
a	r	e
	e	

	e	
e	m	u
	u	

	a	
a	c	e
	e	

As the square gets bigger, it becomes more difficult to make a 'word square'.

t	r	o	t
r	a	v	e
o	v	e	r
t	e	r	m

Can you now find a way to complete these 4 x 4 grids?

s	n	o	w
n			
o			
w			

	n		
	n		
o	n	c	e
	e		

f	l	o	g
l			
o			
g			

l		v	
o	v	e	r
		r	

d	a	f	t
a	b	l	e
f	l		
t	e		

Try to make some grids of your own.

10 Things Found in a ...

The task for the children is to write a simple list poem of 10 things that they might find in a bag/ box of their choice, whether it be a make-up bag, handbag, sports bag or a magic box, jewellery box or even a toolbox.

List poems are easy to write and can be a lot of fun. Make them more interesting by including adjectives, adverbs, similes and metaphors.

The website **www.gigglepoetry.com** has lots of great ideas. See what they've got on list poems by going to the website, clicking on Poetry class and 'What Bugs Me!' Poem.

Find more list poems written by children at **www.poetryzone.co.uk**.

The poet Paul Cookson uses list poems extensively in his work. See for yourself at **www.paulcooksonpoet.co.uk** or book him to perform at your school – fantastic fun!

Many adaptations can be used as extension exercises.

10 Things Found in a ...

What might you find in a Burglar's Swag Bag?

- An escape route!

- A balaclava as dark as his heart!

- A big juicy steak – tasty enough to silence even the fiercest guard dog!

What might a pirate keep in his chest/casket?

Your task is to write a simple list poem of 10 things that you might find in the bag of your choice.

Make your list poem more interesting by including adjectives, adverbs, similes and metaphors.

Use the templates on the following page to create your own list poem case!

What might your heroes carry in their luggage? Or carry with them on tour?

What might the Queen carry in her handbag?

What would you expect to find in David Beckham's kit bag?

What about the Prime Minister?
Your teacher?
Your idol?

10 Things Found in a ...

Use the cut-out templates to make a bag that will contain your list poem folded up inside. Cut around the outside and fold along the dotted lines. Decorate your bag with things that you like.

Write your poem on a piece of paper 7cm wide by 20cm long or use the one to the right. Fold it concertina style into five equal pieces as shown. Glue it inside your bag. Don't forget to add illustrations.

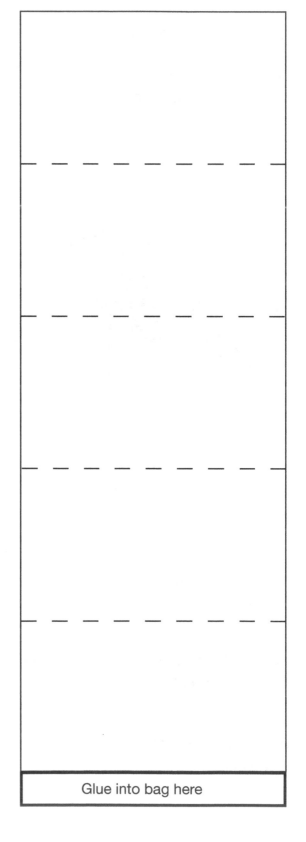

Glue into bag here

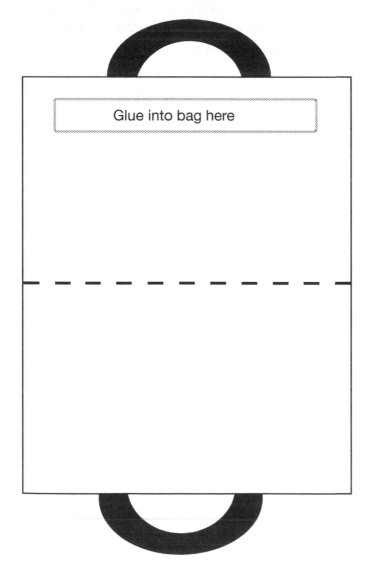

Glue into bag here

© Giles Hughes and Brilliant Publications
Creative Homework Tasks, 7–9 Year Olds

How to Make Your Teacher Very Angry!

The task for the children is to write a simple set of instructions detailing how to make their teacher angry. The children should aim to organize their ideas as an instructive text. It should begin with a heading. For example, 'How to Make Mr Smith Go Crazy!', 'How to Make Mrs Jones Blow her Top!'

This should be followed by a short introduction. For example, 'Follow these simple instructions and send your teacher absolutely mad!'

Next, a sub-heading – 'List of Equipment'. Bullet point a list of what will be needed. Add items like 'a cheeky grin' or 'a voice like a foghorn' for comic effect.

Follow this with another sub-heading – 'What do do'. This should be a numbered list of instructions in chronological order. Use time connectives to link the instructions together – 'firstly, later, next, finally'. The events in the list should get progressively worse so that the teacher finally loses it at home time!

Finally, a concluding paragraph should sum up or reinforce the end result. For example, 'Follow these instructions and you will ensure that your teacher explodes like a volcano before the day is out.'

How to Make Your Teacher Very Angry!

Are there certain things that really annoy your teacher?

Do you know exactly how to wind them up? Does your teacher have pet hates that send them over the edge?

Your task is to write a simple set of instructions. For example, 'How to Make Mrs Jones Blow her Top!'

Then make a list of equipment you will need. For example: 'An extra loud voice, a very leaky handwriting pen, a cheeky grin, a pocket full of stink bombs.'

Next write a numbered list of instructions. Try to put them in chronological order through the school day (use time connectives like: firstly, next and later).

Finally write a sentence that says what the effect will be. For example: 'follow these simple instructions and you're guaranteed to make your teacher explode by home time!'

© Giles Hughes and Brilliant Publications
Creative Homework Tasks, 7–9 Year Olds

Guess Who?

The task for the children is to generate a list of clues about a person in their class or school or even a member of staff, by which someone else could identify them.

Tell the children they can select some clues from the list on page 16, or even make up some of their own. When they get back into school, these can be tested out on their friends to see whether they manage to guess the mystery person!

Encourage the children to produce an A4 sheet of illustrated clues for the person they are describing.

In class use these sheets to run a 'Guess Who?' competition. The children have to match the clues to individuals in their class.

Get the authors to justify their choices and explain why they made their decisions.

As an introduction or extension to the task, divide the class into small groups. Ask each group to produce a 'Guess Who?' list on one of the teaching staff.

Each group can then read out their clues for you to make a guess.

Guess Who?

Think of someone who is in you class or in your school, or even a member of staff.

You are going to write a list of clues for someone to guess who you have chosen.

Select some clues from the list below, or make up some of your own. When you get back to school, you can test these out on your friends to see whether they manage to guess your mystery person!

If this person was an animal, what animal would they be?

If this person was a colour, what colour would they be?

If this person was a type of weather, what kind of weather would they be?

If this person was a type of food, what kind of food would they be?

If this person was a drink, what drink would they be?

If this person was a car, what car would they be?

If this person was a house, what kind of house would they be?

If this person was a song, what song would they be?

If this person was a pop group, what pop group would they be?

If this person was a sweet or chocolate, what sweet or chocolate would they be?

Illustrate your list of clues with matching pictures.

© Giles Hughes and Brilliant Publications
Creative Homework Tasks, 7–9 Year Olds

Kennings

Introduce Kennings to your class with the free powerpoint at:
www.primaryresource.co.uk/english/powerpoint/Kennings.ppt

Kennings are easy to link to work on adverts. This Kenning was used in a famous 1970's advert for Pepsi Cola.

Lipsmackin'
     Thirstquenchin'
         Acetastin'
            Motivatin'
       Goodbuzzin'
     Highwalkin'
Fastlivin'
     Evergivin
       Coolfizzin'

Kennings

Kennings were used a lot in Celtic and Viking stories. A kenning is a way of describing something without saying what it is. For example, **a tail wagger** could be a **dog**.

It is easy to write a poem by using a list of kennings.

Can you guess what these Kennings Poems are describing?

Kennings 1

>   A bird dresser
>   A pillow filler
>   An arrow maker
>   A dust tamer
>   A cobweb-breaker
>   A tickle maker

_____

Kennings 2

>   A fur lump
>   A secret listener
>   A hole digger
>   A swift hopper
>   A currant dropper
>   A carrot nibbler

_____

Kennings 3

>   A round facer
>   A still stander
>   A two hander
>   A heart beater
>   A sudden shrieker
>   A time keeper

_____

Write and illustrate some kennings of your own.

If you need some ideas for the theme of your poem, try these … .

… your teacher

… your pet

…your Mum or Dad

… your best friend

… your favourite music artist or group

Answers: *Kennings 1 = a feather. Kennings 2 = a rabbit. Kennings 3 - a clock.*

© Giles Hughes and Brilliant Publications
Creative Homework Tasks, 7–9 Year Olds

Plotting Points

Reinforce the points of the compass and ask the children to follow the instructions carefully and in order. If completed correctly the children should produce a picture of an elephant:

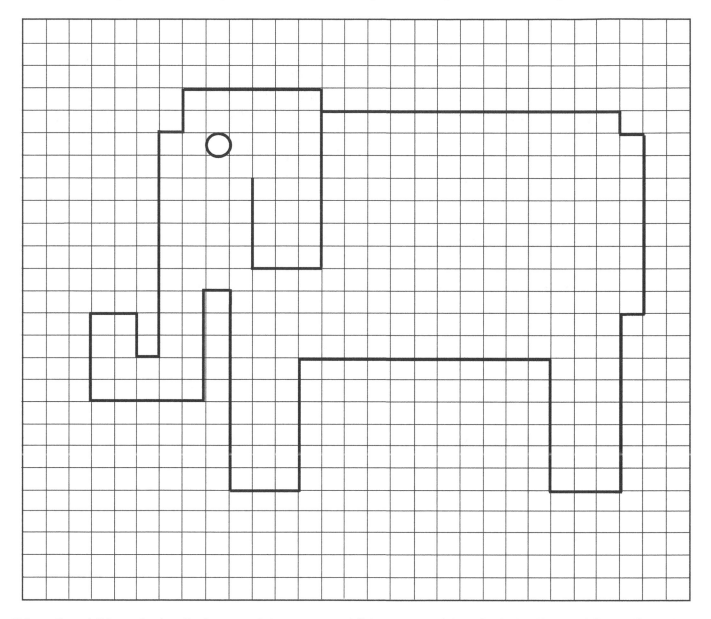

When the children design their own picture, some children may wish to include diagonal lines. If so, they may need to be introduced to other points of the compass.

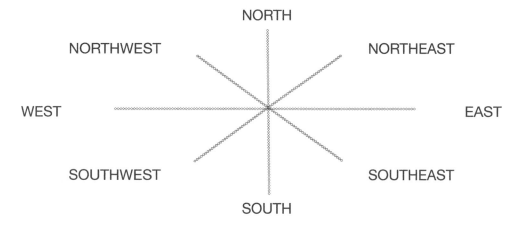

Plotting Points

Use the usual points of the compass to plot these points in order. Join them up to draw an animal shape. Follow the instructions carefully.

Start at Point X
Go 4 squares south
3 squares east
8 squares north
6 squares west
2 square south
1 square west
10 squares south
1 square west
2 square north
2 square west

4 squares south
5 squares east
5 squares north
1 square east
9 squares south
3 squares east
6 squares north
11 squares east
6 squares south
3 squares east

8 squares north
1 square east
8 squares north
1 square west
1 square north
13 squares west

What aminal have
you drawn?

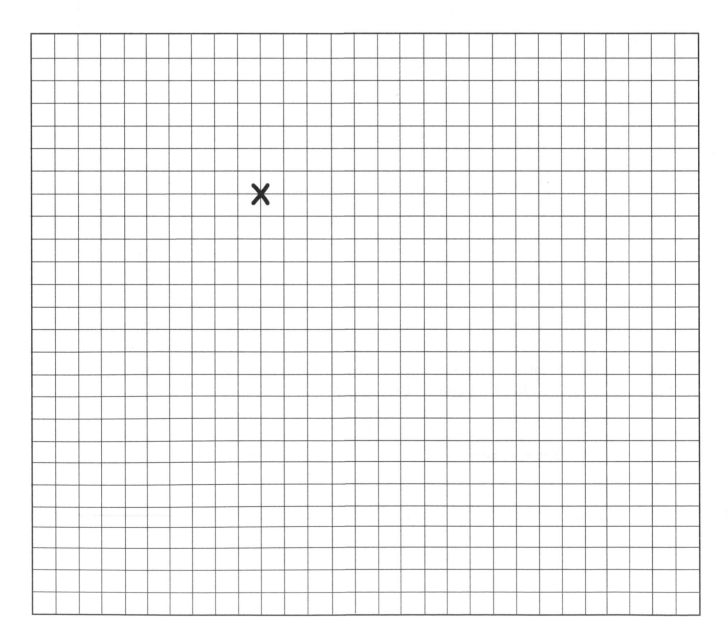

© Giles Hughes and Brilliant Publications
Creative Homework Tasks, 7–9 Year Olds

Plotting Points

Now try designing one of your own.

Firstly draw a picture on the grid.

Only use straight lines.

If you want to draw diagonal lines, you will need to use more points of the compass.

Then write the instructions to draw your shape in the correct order.

Back at school you can swop your instructions with a friend to see if you can both complete each other's drawings from the instructions given.

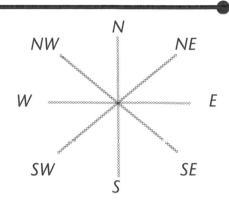

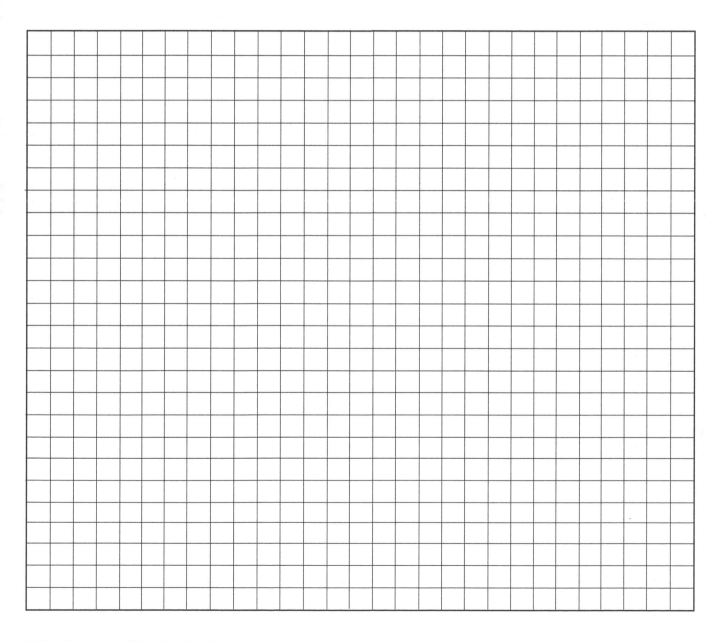

Odd One Out

Hand the children the homework sheets on pages 23 and 24 and set the task of finding the odd one out. When challenging the children to devise their own 'odd one out' questions, try relating it to their topic work. For example, 'Write five odd one out questions about the Tudors' or 'Make up some odd one out questions about forces'.

Answers to homework tasks:

The **Dalmatian** is the odd one out as it is a dog, all the others are cats.

The **bat** is the odd one out as it is a mammal, all the others are birds.

Toronto is the odd one out as it is a Canadian city, all the others are American cities.

The **parrot** is the odd one out as it is the only bird that can fly.

Badminton is the odd one out as it is played with a shuttlecock, all the others use a ball.

The **cube** is the odd one out as it is the only 3-D shape.

The **spider** is the odd one out as it is an arachnoid, all the others are insects.

The **xylophone** is the odd one out as all the others are stringed instruments.

Smoke is the odd one out, all the others are forms of water.

The **shark** is the odd one out as it is a fish, all the others are mammals.

© Giles Hughes and Brilliant Publications
Creative Homework Tasks, 7–9 Year Olds

Odd One Out

Can you work out which one is the odd one out? Don't forget to say why!

Cat	Lion	Dalmation	Tiger	Odd one out	Reason

Bat	Crow	Heron	Thrush	Odd one out	Reason

New York	Toronto	Washington	Chicago	Odd one out	Reason

Ostrich	Kiwi	Penguin	Parrot	Odd one out	Reason

Table-tennis	Squash	Tennis	Badminton	Odd one out	Reason

Kite	Rectangle	Octagon	Cube	Odd one out	Reason

Butterfly	Bee	Spider	Ant	Odd one out	Reason

Odd One Out

Violin	Cello	Xylophone	Guitar	Odd one out	Reason
Steam	Smoke	Ice	Water	Odd one out	Reason
Dolphin	Shark	Sea Lion	Whale	Odd one out	Reason

Now have a go and make some of your own!

				Odd one out	Reason
				Odd one out	Reason
				Odd one out	Reason

© Giles Hughes and Brilliant Publications
Creative Homework Tasks, 7–9 Year Olds

Elf Towers!

The Elves are designing and building a new high-rise development in Elf Town! This will consist of four-storey, three-storey and two-storey towers. Ask the children to think about how many different designs they could come up with using black and white blocks only. Encourage the children to be systematic in their approach, for example work out all towerblocks containing three black sections first, then two black sections and finally one black section.

There are 16 different towers using four blocks.

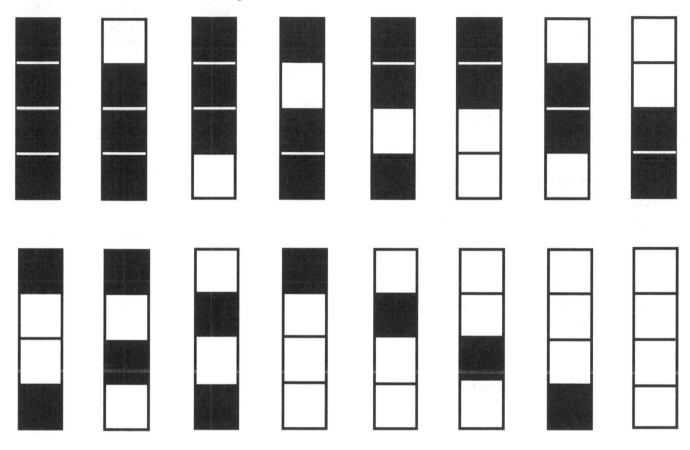

There are 8 possible designs using three blocks and only four options possible using two blocks.

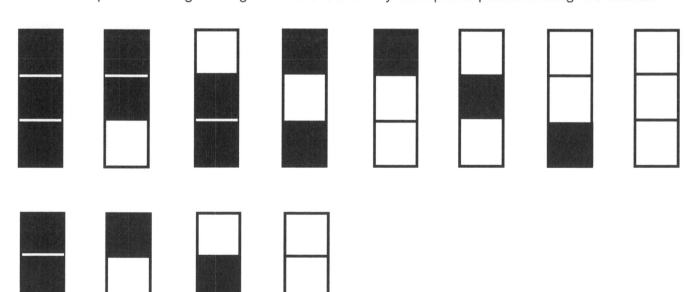

Elf Towers!

The elves are building a new high-rise development in Elf Town!

The elves asked an architect to design some black and white towers for them; they are afraid of heights and do not want any of the towers to be more than four blocks high. The architect came up with these tower blocks!

The elves were so happy with the towers that they ordered a complete set of towers, each four blocks high, and they wanted each one to be different!

Your task is to make a list of all the different four block towers that are possible! The towers can only be made from black or white blocks.

Some older elves are not as fit as they used to be and can only manage towers with three blocks. Can you design a set of towers for them?

Is it possible to have different towers of just

two blocks?

Draw out all the possible design options.

© Giles Hughes and Brilliant Publications
Creative Homework Tasks, 7–9 Year Olds

Mental Maths Machine

The mental maths machines work in the same way as fortune tellers.

The printed example contains a variety of mathematical operations and vocabulary. It is easy to simplify a machine so that it only uses information from the six times table, for example.

Used in this way, you could put a mental maths machine together each week, concentrating on a particular times table.

Instead of spelling words out as the machine is opened and closed, children can 'chant' a times table. For example: 5 – 10 – 15 – 20.

Try sketching 2-D and 3-D shapes on each section of the mental maths machine – challenge children to work out the number of sides, edges, flat surfaces, verticals, curved surfaces, faces etc.

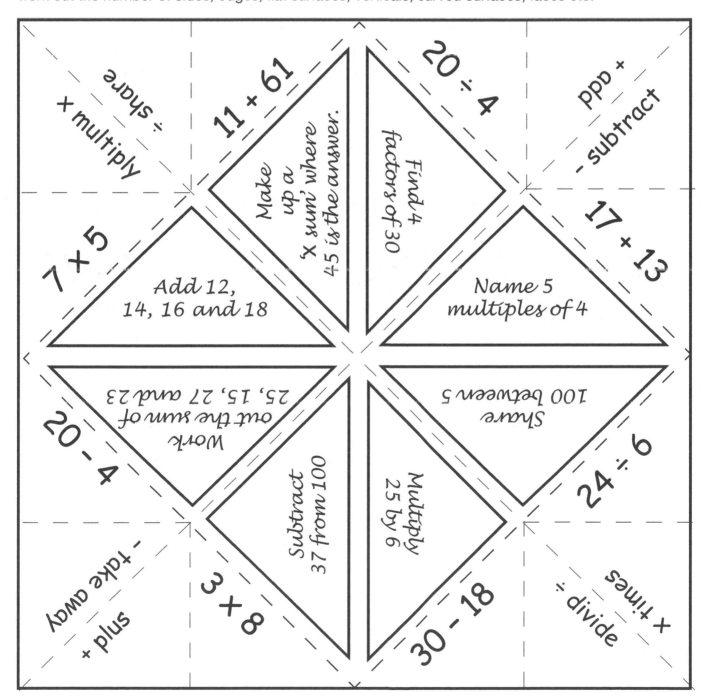

Mental Maths Machine

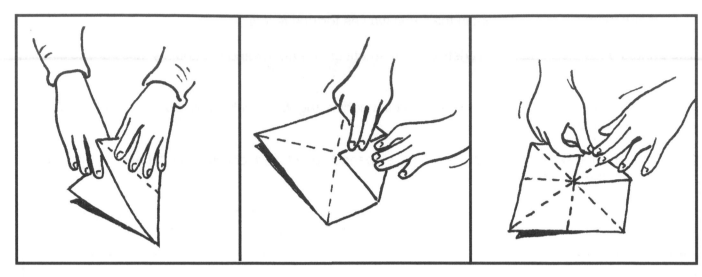

1. Cut out the mental maths machine. Lay it printed side down, then fold and crease along both diagonals.

2. Fold in each of the 4 corners so they meet at the centre point.

3. Turn it over and lay it on the table. Fold in the 4 corners again so that they too meet at the centre point.

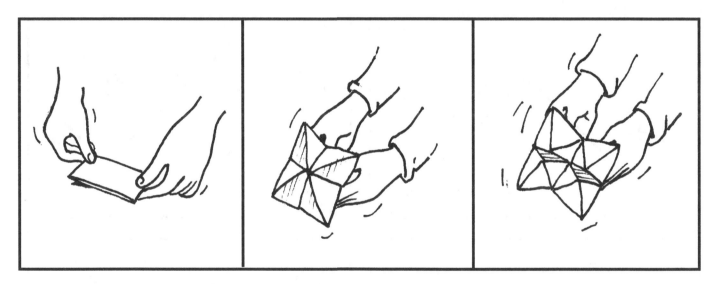

4. Fold the top edge down to meet the bottom edge, crease the fold and unfold again. Fold the right side to meet the left side and crease. Unfold again.

5. Hold it up as shown above and slip your thumb and index finger from both hands under the square flaps at the back, pinching the folds.

6. Practise opening and closing the 'mouth'. Now you are ready to challenge you friends.

Hold the mental maths machine in both forefingers and thumbs, in the way described on the instruction sheet. Demonstrate to the children how it works.

Ask a friend to choose one of the eight operations written around the top of the mental maths machine.

Spell out the word, moving the 'mouth', first one way and then the other.

Next ask your friend to work out one of the sums shown.

If they answer correctly, lift the flap and challenge them to answer in 10 seconds.

© Giles Hughes and Brilliant Publications
Creative Homework Tasks, 7–9 Year Olds

Mental Maths Machine

Here is a blank mental maths machine. Cut it out and fold it as described on the instruction sheet. Write some mental maths problems of your own in each section. Try it out on your friends and family!

House of the Future

The task for the children is to design a house for the future, taking into consideration environmental factors.

Talk about how technology has progressed and how this has led to environmental changes in both our life-styles and the world around us. Maybe because of climate change or even space exploration, we will need to change the design of our houses. Discuss the different scenarios and hence different ideas for designs of houses of the future.

Remind the children that they may wish to consider the following when planning a new house design: location, materials available, water supply, waste disposal and sanitation, energy sources, sizes required, transport links, security and communication networks/systems.

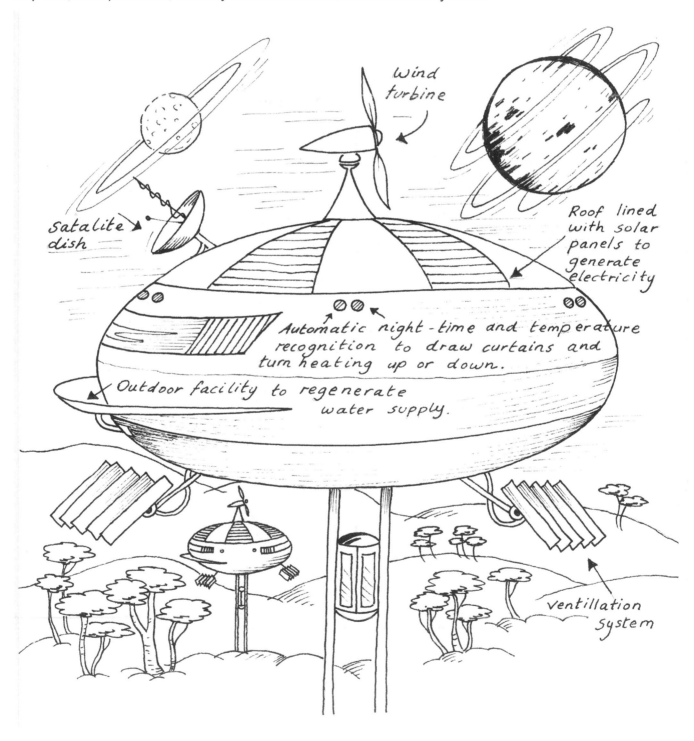

Wind turbine

Satalite dish

Roof lined with solar panels to generate electricity

Automatic night-time and temperature recognition to draw curtains and turn heating up or down.

Outdoor facility to regenerate water supply.

ventillation system

House of the Future

What do you think the house of the future might look like?

Draw your design and label any unusual or interesting features!

Planet earth may get over crowded in the future if sea levels rise and if the population continues to increase! Where will people live then? In floating homes? Maybe beneath the ocean? Perhaps in underground homes? Or could our tower blocks get taller? Because of a lack of materials, we might be forced to build new houses entirely from re-cycled objects!

Maybe in the distant future we will be living on other planets or moons! How might these houses look?

New School Uniform

The task for the children is to design a new school uniform to wear while attending their school on Mars.

Talk about 'Life on Mars', and how the uniform must conform to certain criteria. Don't forget to tell them about the 'Nibblers'.

The planet is swarming with Martians, we've called Nibblers. These are dangerous creatures known to attack humans whenever possible. Nibblers are small with very sharp teeth. Luckily their eyesight is very poor and they have no sense of smell. As they were here before us, it has been deemed illegal to kill them. So, we have to do our best to co-exist alongside them! However, they can be repelled with water.

Encourage the children to draw both front and back views of their uniform, and to label the special features. It will need compartments to hold their belongings and will also need breathing apparatus. The uniform might also benefit from being camouflaged – remember the Nibblers have poor eyesight and may miss red uniforms against a red landscape.

They will need to select a material that is warm or incorporate a heating system into the uniform.

It must be rugged and hard wearing to cope with the terrain – try using kneepads, elbow pads, etc. It will also need a helmet of some kind.

The children will also need to design a school badge or logo for the school and incorporate it into their design.

And finally, as the Nibblers are small, it could be that long 'bite-proof' boots would be an advantage. The alien's aversion to water might mean the children design a sprinkler system or have some kind of water pistol as a feature.

New School Uniform

Your task is to design a new school uniform. This will be a school uniform with a difference. The children who wear it go to school on the planet Mars!

Points to consider:

- The children will need to walk to school in their uniform.

- The atmosphere on Mars is mostly made up of carbon dioxide. There is not enough oxygen to breathe.

- Mars in known as the red planet.

- Mars is very cold compared to Earth.

- Mars is covered in craters and mountains; the landscape is very barren and rocky.

- The children will need to carry their books, PE kit and lunch boxes to school.

- The uniform must be smart, comfortable and practical.

Warning!

The planet is swarming with Martians, we've called Nibblers. These are dangerous creatures known to attack humans whenever possible. Nibblers are small with very sharp teeth. Luckily their eyesight is very poor and they have no sense of smell. As they were here before us, it has been deemed illegal to kill them. So, we have to do our best to co-exist alongside them! However, they can be repelled with water.

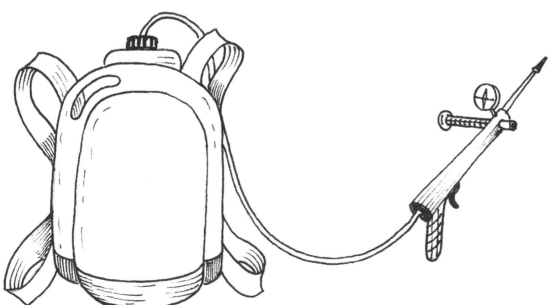

Escape!

The task for the children is to design a 'James Bond' style gadget watch. Talk about some of 'James Bond's' gadgets or even 'Inspector Gadget's' gadgets.

'Laser gun' – This mini laser gun beams out a red-hot laser beam. Use it to cut your way out of the wooden hut!

'Sleeping potion' – The gas powered dart is full of fast action sleeping potion. Use it to knock the guard out!

'Shark repellent' – Screw out this tiny glass vial. Once in the water, break the glass; the chemicals in the vial will ensure no sharks will attack you!

'Skeleton key' – Screw out of the watch and use to pick the lock of the handcuffs.

'Ultra high/sonic frequency sound' too high for humans but guard dogs will stay out of your way!

Are there any female versions out there? Special fragrances that cause only men to black out?

Ask the children to use their imagination to invent a watch that will cater for all their needs. And don't forget to label them!

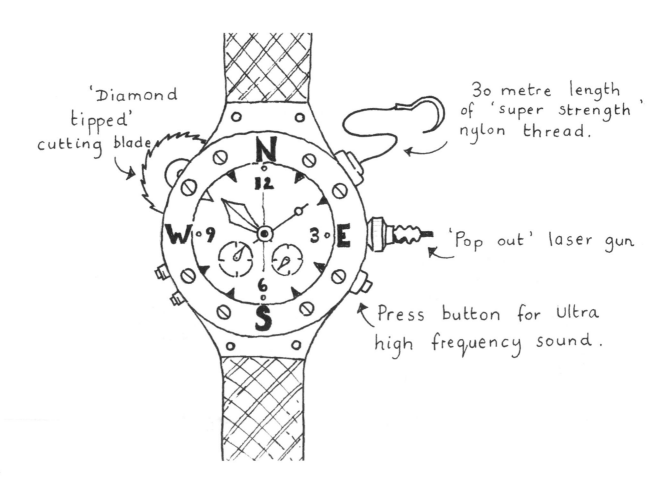

Escape!

Imagine you are a spy who has been captured. You are being held captive on a tiny island that is surrounded by shark-infested waters. Handcuffed in a small wooden hut, you are being guarded by an enemy agent and his two vicious dogs!

Design a watch with gadgets that will help you to escape! Sketch and label your design. Explain how the gadgets will help you to escape!

Try making your watch from card, wear it to school and tell your friends how the gadgets help you!

Design a Robo-pet!

The children's task is to design their own labour-saving robo-pet.

Discuss the advantages of having your very own Robo-pet. What can it do? Encourage the children to think of some useful functions like the ones below:

- Simply add water to one ear funnel, and milk to the other this robo-pet will do the rest … a cup of tea served to perfection (parents will love it!)

- Tea pours out of a 'tea shoot'

- Robo-pet glides silently on a cushion of air, just like a hovercraft! (No noise to annoy Mum!)

- Fires tennis balls and cricket balls out of the tail. Great for keeping fit or if there is no-one to play with!

- Built-in games console and CD player

- Mini flat screen TV with DVD

- Robo-pet has built in Hoover so it sucks up dirt, fluff and dust as it moves around the house. One less job for Mum!

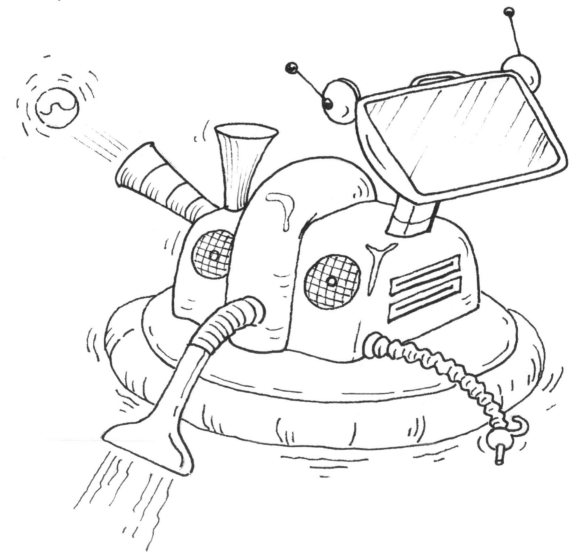

Design a Robo-pet!

You have been pestering your mum for a new pet and finally she has cracked!

Because Mum refused to hoover up any animal hairs, buy any pet food or scoop up any poop, you are only left with one option – a Robo-pet!

Your parents will only allow you a Robo-pet as long as:

- It doesn't take up too much space

- It's designed to do at least two of Mum's household chores

- It will keep you occupied (robo-pets are expensive and this toy will have to last!)

- It looks good! Mum would hate to be shown up in public with an embarrassing pet!

Design a robo-pet that meets all Mum's needs and all your needs!

Draw and label your robo-pet.

Explain how it will keep you occupied.

Explain how it will help Mum out.

Make sure that all the gadgets and features are clearly labelled.

Make additional sketches if you need to.

Don't forget to give your robo-pet a name and make sure it looks good!

Transforming Natural Patterns

The children's task is to take a pattern from nature and transform it for use as a decoration on an everyday object.

There are thousands of fantastic patterns found in nature: from tree bark and leaves, to the skin types/ feathers found on animals and birds, through to rock formations and clouds.

Encourage the children to take a natural pattern and extend or repeat it. They should sketch the pattern as a 'before' and 'after' transformation.

If you want to investigate more natural patterns, type 'natural patterns' into any search engine. The top choice is usually Ian Alexander's Natural Pattern Library. This is a fantastic site that children love to explore. It contains hundreds of truly weird and wonderful natural patterns. Why not print off a selection and transform them!

As an extension to this exercise look at wallpaper design. Can the children design their own wallpaper?

Transforming Natural Patterns

There are thousands of fantastic patterns found in nature.

This is what alligator skin looks like:

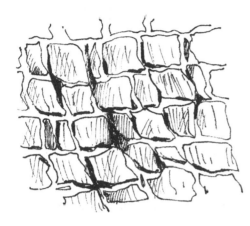

What can you transform this piece of alligator skin into?

Does it remind you of anything?

What does it look like?

What could you transform it into?

With a little imagination it could become…

An old ladies' handbag.

This is a Mollusc sea shell. How can you transform it?

Haunted House

The task for the children is to design a haunted house with opening flaps.

For inspiration and ideas try reading and showing the children the pop-up book *Haunted House* by Jan Pienkowski.

Before starting their own *haunted house* designs, the children should sketch out their ideas – this will help them to organize their designs.

The haunted house illustration can be put together in two different ways:
1.   Draw what the house looks like from the outside first. With a craft knife, the children can cut away 3 sides of the flaps they wish to open. Their design will need to be glued to a blank piece of paper so that the scenes behind the flaps can be drawn on.

2.   Draw the house, but where a flap will be – draw the scene that will lie beneath it. The flaps will then need to be made separately and carefully glued in place.

The second method requires more initial planning but means that craft knives will not be used.

As an extension task, drawing 'What happens next' scenes, encourages the children to think about story lines and where to put possible windows to bring excitement into the picture. Could the children draw an exciting 'What happens next' scene to their haunted house? Does a huge big bat fly out of the chimney? Or a skeleton open the door? Or even a monster plant tangle itself around some poor person's legs?

Haunted House

Your task is to design and draw a Haunted House!

Your haunted house design should have a number of flaps that can be opened and closed to reveal 'special features' that a haunted house would have.

Flaps can be perfect for revealing cut away views and showing what is inside something, like in this …

An easy solution is to use flaps for doors and windows in houses and buildings.

Try designing your own pictures that have flaps which reveal "what happens next", like with this picture here!

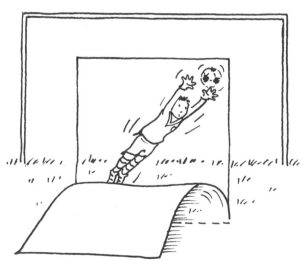

Changes

The task for the children is to draw of series of pictures showing the stages of how a piece of food changes as it is eaten.

Firstly, you need to select the food to be drawn. Choose a medium that suits the food.

Drawing biscuits in pencil gives good results. Choose a biscuit with a pattern and/or writing. Rich tea and digestive biscuits work particularly well. Draw an apple, peach or similar fruit with coloured chalk or pastel. An open sandwich is effective when drawn lightly in pencil and then coloured with watercolours or watercolour pencils. Try drawing a banana being peeled and eaten, ending with just the skin remaining.

How many pictures do the children need to draw? Some children favour plotting out a grid of six or eight squares to show the changes. However, showing just three or four pictures in a straight line can be very effective.

Encourage the children to include as much detail as possible, showing crumbs and even teeth marks.

Similar work could be undertaken over a period of days on the theme of decay of an apple core, for example, or a banana.

If this task was carried out at Halloween time, the children could hollow out pumpkins to create horror faces in the traditional way. In succeeding days drawings could be made showing the gradual decay of the pumpkin and the changing nature of the face created.

Changes

Complete a series of drawings to show how a piece of food changes as it is eaten. For example a biscuit.

This biscuit is being eaten slowly! Each drawing shows a different stage.

What food will you choose to eat and draw? Try an apple, a piece of cake, a banana or make a sandwich!

You should draw your chosen food as a whole first, take a bite and then draw each different stage you see as you slowly eat it.

Top tips for a great picture!
Remember to show details like teeth marks.

Think about what medium is best suited to draw the food you have chosen. Will you do a simple line drawing in pencil or would coloured pencils or even watercolours be more effective?

What will your last picture show – an empty plate, crumbs, a screwed up wrapper or an apple core and pips?

How many pictures will you need in your series of drawings?

How will you set out your pictures – in a straight line across or down or maybe in a grid?

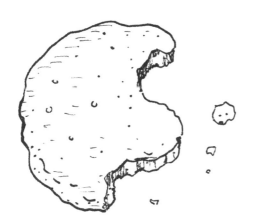

Robot Collage!

To design and make a robot collage using objects cut from a photocopied sheet.

The resource sheet for this activity is made up from images taken from Victorian times (page 36, one sheet per child for their robot collage). This activity also works well using photocopied objects. Metallic objects like tools and cutlery photocopy best, or use kitchenware from magazines/newspapers/ advertisements. Every photocopier is different and you will need to experiment with the light/dark control to get the clearest definition. Try enlarging and reducing objects for effect.

The children might find it helpful to sketch a rough design before they begin. Encourage them to design creatively, considering different body shapes, limb arrangements and facial features for their robots.

Ask the children to carefully cut out a large selection of objects and shapes before they begin the task. (Accurately cut pieces look far more effective than carelessly cut pieces.)

The robots look most effective when whole items are pieced together. Discourage the children from cutting things like eyes, mouth or head shapes from their photocopies.

When gluing down the pieces, use a clear setting glue like Pritt Stick® or PVA. Avoid smudges as a clean, clear cut collage is far more attractive.

.

Robot Collage!

You are going to design and make a collage of your own robot. Carefully cut out the objects on the photocopied sheet. Look at them closely, select some appropriate pieces and make a pencil sketch of your robot design.

Be adventurous when designing your robot – it doesn't need to have legs – can you think of another way for the robot to move about? Not all robots need to have two eyes or even eyes at all!

Work on one part of the robot at a time. Start from the top/head, move on to the main body/torso and finally add any limbs or attachments you may wish to include in your design.

Try to use the whole piece of the object, don't be tempted to cut eye or mouth shapes from the photocopy – try to find a piece that resembles the feature you need!

Glue the pieces down carefully as dirty smudges can ruin the effect.

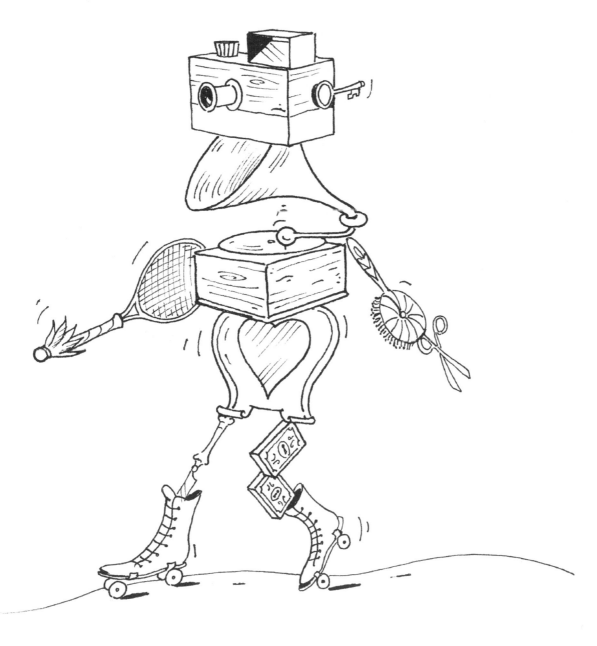

Robot Collage!

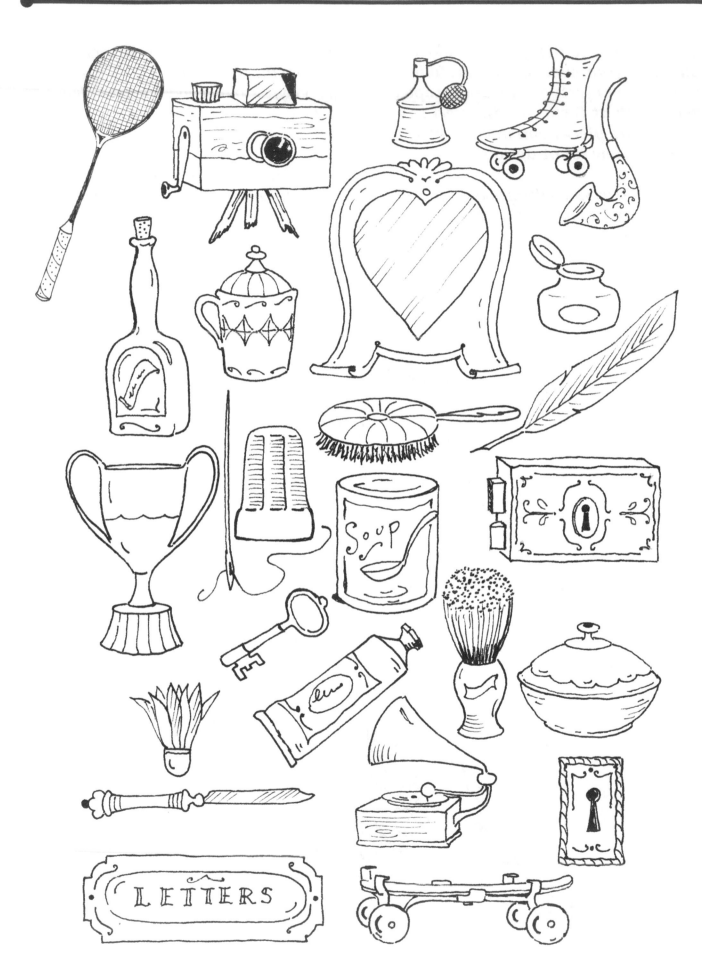

© Giles Hughes and Brilliant Publications
Creative Homework Tasks, 7–9 Year Olds

Number Transformations

The task for the children is to be creative and doodle with numbers.

For inspiration on how numbers and letters can be transformed, search Google images for 'Doodle 4 Google'. Here you will find lots of images created by children who have transformed the Google logo, it's well worth a visit!

Creative Homework Tasks, 7–9 Year Olds

Number Transformations

Look at the number three. See the ways it has been transformed into other images.

Write the numbers 1 to 10

Transform each number into something imaginative and interesting ... be creative!

Write your name in capital letters. Can you transform the letters of your name into something about you, your family, your hobbies and interests?

© Giles Hughes and Brilliant Publications
Creative Homework Tasks, 7–9 Year Olds

Bird's-eye View

Show the children what a bird's-eye view is. Prepare and show samples.

There are plenty of extension tasks or further challenges for this activity. Link the task to the children's favourite book. Try a bird's-eye view of Horrid Henry's bedroom, Mr Twit's kitchen or the BFG's cave!

The children could draw bird's-eye views of their school site, their classroom or their perfect classroom.

Give the task an imaginative twist by drawing a bird's-eye view of a theme park, an alien city or the living quarters on a space ship.

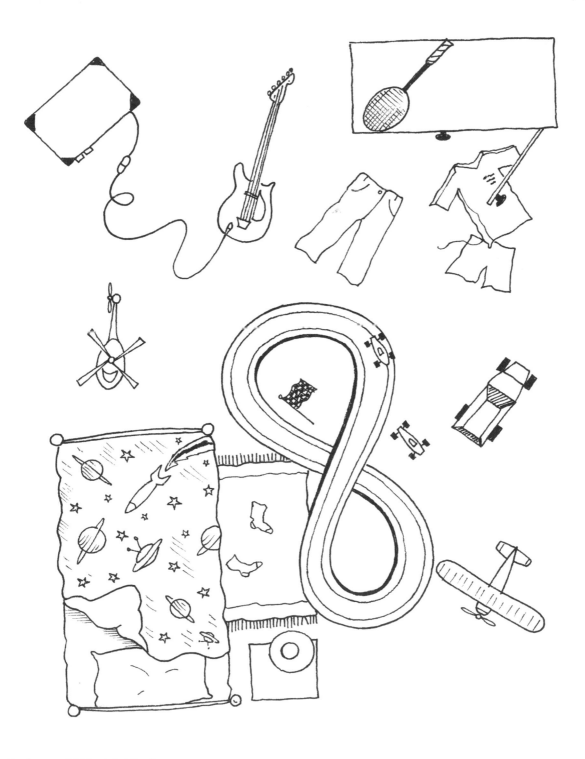

Bird's-Eye View

Imagine that you are on the ceiling looking down at your bedroom. What would you see?

Draw and label a bird's eye plan of your bedroom. Include details like piles of smelly socks in the corner or old toys and comics piled on top of your wardrobe!

Remember that you are drawing things from above so objects may look different.

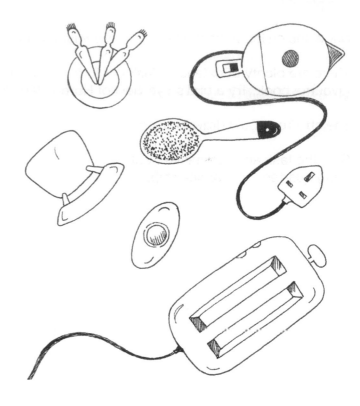

© Giles Hughes and Brilliant Publications
Creative Homework Tasks, 7–9 Year Olds

Design an African Mask

The children have the task of designing and making an African war mask using card and paper.

You could supply the children with a simple template, with pre-cut eyeholes and string attached. They can then build their design around this.

For inspiration, the children could investigate more African masks at **www.authenticafrica.com**.

A very child-friendly website is **www.artyfactory.com/africanmasks/index.html**. There is a wealth of information and examples at this site which also contains a step-by-step guide to designing a really effective two-tone African mask.

When the children complete their masks and bring them back to school, try putting pupils into small groups and challenge them to devise a war dance that they can perform to their classmates.

Search YouTube for examples of war dances to show your children – the New Zealand Maori 'Haka' always goes down well!

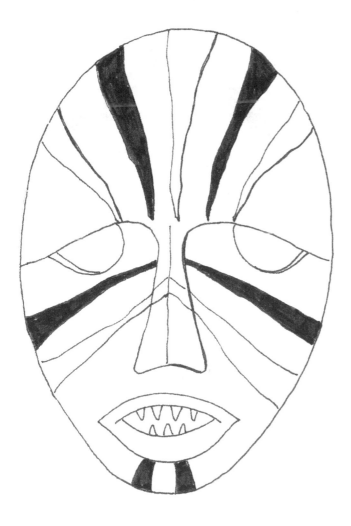

Design an African Mask

Your task is to design and make an African mask using card and paper. The mask you design is going to be a War Mask!

Your mask should make you look as fierce and frightening as possible, so that it will strike fear into your enemies when you go into battle!

You might need to exaggerate features on your mask to make it look truly terrifying!

- *A large mouth with huge, sharp teeth might help!*
- *Wild, glaring eyes would look alarming!*
- *Try making spiked hair or add horns and tusks!*
- *Add stylized scars and tattoos for extra effect!*

Remember that you will need to wear your mask. Make sure it has eye holes you can see through, is comfortable to wear and you can breathe when you wear it.

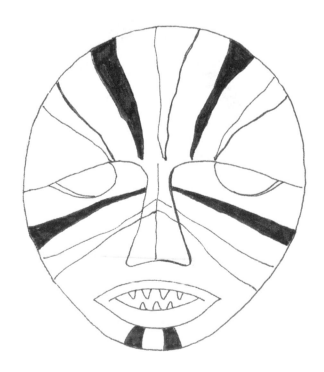

 www.brilliantpublications.co.uk

© Giles Hughes and Brilliant Publications
Creative Homework Tasks, 7–9 Year Olds

Sahara Survival

The task for the children is to pack a rucksack for desert survival.

Challenge your children to find out which countries are in the Sahara desert.

There are eleven countries in total: Algeria, Chad, Egypt, Libya, Mali, Mauritania, Morocco, Niger, Sudan, Tunisia, and Western Sahara.

There are numerous animals that live in the Sahara desert. How many can the children find?

The animals include dromedary camels, goats, scorpions, monitor lizards, cheetahs, ostrich, sand vipers, cobras, mongoose, jackal, sand fox, spotted hyena, gerbil, cape hare and desert hedgehog!

Sahara Survival

The Sahara desert is in North West Africa, where it is very hot and dry!

The Sahara holds the world record for the hottest place on Earth ... an amazing 58°C in the shade!

At night the Sahara desert becomes very cold, with temperatures falling below freezing!

Strong desert winds can cause sand to form tornadoes!

Few plants grow in the desert and only hardy animals survive!

Your mission is to pack a rucksack with items that might help you to survive in the Sahara desert!

Draw your chosen items around the rucksack on the worksheet. Write an explanation for each of your choices.

Think about:
    Heat
    Sunshine
    Water
    Shade
    Cold
    Sleeping
    Wild life
    Travelling
    Dangers
    Recording your experiences

© Giles Hughes and Brilliant Publications
Creative Homework Tasks, 7–9 Year Olds

Sahara Survival

What will you pack in your bag? Use the back of this sheet if you need more room.

Fossil Fact File

The task for the children is to cut out and piece together the bones on page 57 (enlarge and photocopy this page, one for each child), and stick them down on a new piece of paper.

The second part of this challenge is for the children, using the Fossil Fact File pages 58 and 59, to draw and write a description about a new breed of dinosaur that they have just discovered.

When introducing this task, it is a good idea to talk through the 'Fossil Fact File' with the class. The following list gives a few starting points to spark conversation, ideas and imagination.

Name of dinosaur: Try to think of something different – if your dinosaur was slow moving, why not call it 'Plod-o-saurus' or 'Shuffle-o-saurus'.

Size of dinosaur: Be realistic – find out the biggest and smallest known dinosaurs. Don't make yours 100 metres tall!

Weight of dinosaur: Heavy things can't fly! If yours is a flying dinosaur, make it light. If it is a very light animal, it might struggle to attack and kill bigger animals unless it hunts in packs or has a venomous bite.

Speed of dinosaur: The fastest human can only run at about 25 mph. A cheetah can double that speed. Some fish are very quick swimmers; does your dinosaur live underwater?

Artist's impression: Refer to your skeleton sheet to help you get the right shape. The colours are up to you. Does your dinosaur use camouflage colour like a chameleon?

Eating habits: Is your dinosaur a carnivore, herbivore or omnivore? How does it hunt and kill its prey?

Preferred habitat: Where does it live? The jungle, grasslands, under the sea, up trees, in the desert, etc.

Senses: Pick out any strengths and weaknesses. Does your dinosaur have brilliant eyesight? Can it see well at night? Is it almost blind? Does it have amazing hearing or is it as deaf as a post?

Unusual characteristics: Let your imagination run wild! Can you link any unusual characteristics to the dinosaur's habitat or senses? For example, if your dinosaur lives in a hot desert – it might hop quickly from foot to foot to avoid burning its feed on the hot sand.

Reasons for death: How did your dinosaur die? Was it killed by another dinosaur? Did it starve to death? Did it eat poisoned plants? Did it freeze to death? Was it killed in massive forest wild fires?

Fossil Fact File

Your first task is to piece together the bones. Carefully cut around the bones, re-arrange them to form a pre-historic monster. Stick them down on a new piece of paper. What skeleton have you made?

Fossil Fact File

You are digging in your garden and you find a collection of fossilized bones! You have just discovered a new breed of dinosaur that has never been seen before. Describe it below.

Name of dinosaur:

_____

Size of dinosaur (in cm and m):

_____

Weight (in kg and g):

_____

Speed (in mph):

_____

Artist's impression of dinosaur

Fossil Fact File

Eating habits: _____

_____

_____

Habitat: _____

_____

_____

Senses (strengths and weaknesses): _____

_____

_____

Unusual and interesting characteristics: _____

_____

_____

Reason for death: _____

_____

_____

Laid to Rest

The children's task is to make an Egyptian Shabti sculpture.

Talk about the Egyptian figure called 'Shabti'. They are small human-shaped figures that would represent a person to perform a given task for the deceased in the after-life. Unsurprisingly, wealthy nobles and royalty did not plan on doing any work themselves, so they would take their (symbolic) servants with them. Early versions (Shabti or Ushabti) were modelled to represent the task that they would perform and given tiny tools with which to complete their tasks. Shabti were made from various materials including; faience (a non-clay based ceramic), wax, clay, wood, stone, terracotta and occasionally glass and bronze.

Tell the children that their task is to make an Egyptian shabti statue using clay or Plasticine®, then make a list of the things that they – the children, would want to take into the afterlife.

Don't be put off by offering a homework task involving clay – all the mess will be at home!

It is easier to use air drying clay. This is available from most art and craft suppliers. Traditional school clay becomes brittle when air dried and breaks easily if not fired in a kiln. Although *air drying clay* is better to use, it does dry out quickly and may be unusable by the time the children get it home. The best method would be to cut the clay into small sections and wrap them individually in cling film. These clay bundles can then be handed out at the end of the day with the homework task – no mess!

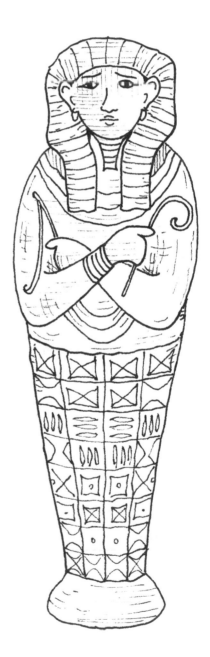

An alternative is to use Plasticine® instead of clay. This way you can get the children to use more than one colour on their shabti statue.

Try getting the children to present their statues to the rest of the class and explain their choice of objects. This makes an excellent circle time activity and throws up many interesting areas for discussion and debate.

© Giles Hughes and Brilliant Publications
Creative Homework Tasks, 7–9 Year Olds

Laid to Rest

The ancient Egyptians believed that when they died they would become immortal.

It was the custom that all Egyptians were buried with objects they would need after death. For some this meant everyday objects such as bowls, combs and other trinkets, along with food. Wealthier Egyptians could afford to be buried with jewellery, furniture and other valuables (this made their tombs targets for robbers!)

In addition, some Egyptians were buried with a small statue called a shabti. They believed that this shabti would perform work for them in the afterlife.

One of the terracotta army

A shabti statue

In ancient China, an Emperor called Shi Huangdi was buried with a huge army of almost ten thousand life-sized pottery soldiers. They are known as the terracotta army. The purpose of the terracotta army was to help Shi Huangdi rule another empire in the afterlife. Some people think that the army was also built for protection.

In ancient England, a King called Raedwald was buried in a place called Sutton Hoo. In 1939 his grave was unearthed. Raedwald had been buried in a huge wooden ship. Around his body were helmets, swords, spears, silver bowls and other treasures. The objects he was buried with tell us about his life, how important he was, what he was famous for and what he thought he would need in the afterlife.

A helmet found at Sutton Hoo

Laid to Rest

Your teacher will give you a small piece of clay or Plasticine® to take home.

Your task is to make it into an Egyptian shabti sculpture of your own!

- *Mould the clay into the shape you want; use tools like old pencils, knives and cocktail sticks to carve and draw details onto your figure*

- *What work do you want your shabti to carry out for you in the afterlife? How will you show this? Think about what the shabti might be wearing or holding. Draw on symbols and signs that give clues to what jobs the shabti will perform*

- *Make a list of the things that you would want to take to the afterlife. Think about what is important to you, what could you do without? What could someone learn about you from the list you make?*

Extension task
The tradition of burying objects with people used to be important to societies all over the world. Now the tradition seems to have died out. Can you think of a reason why this might be?

Talking Heads

The task for the children is to think about their ambitions.

This homework activity can be adapted for use at the beginning of the year. Try giving the activity to your new class in September. Ask the children to 'show your new teacher what you want them to know about you.' This gives the children an opportunity to share their talents, ambitions, strengths and weaknesses in an informal and fun format.

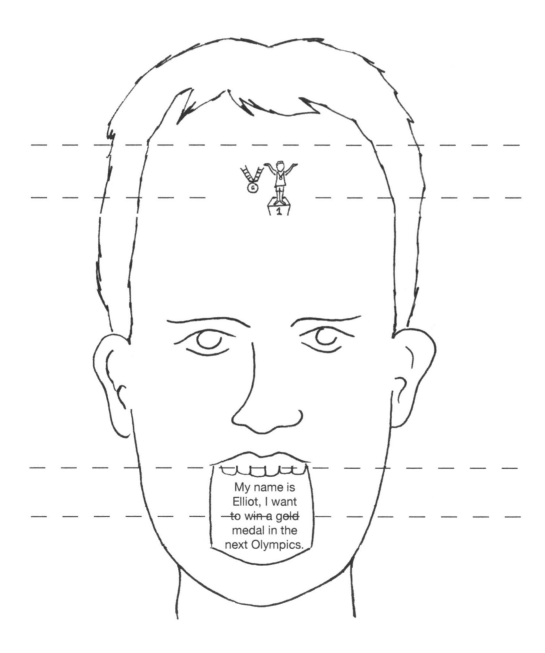

My name is Elliot, I want to win a gold medal in the next Olympics.

Talking Heads

This is Elliot. His likes doing gymnastics at school and his ambition is to become good enough to compete at the next Olympics.

Cut out his 'Talking Head' and then fold along the dotted lines. Fold the paper so it looks like this:

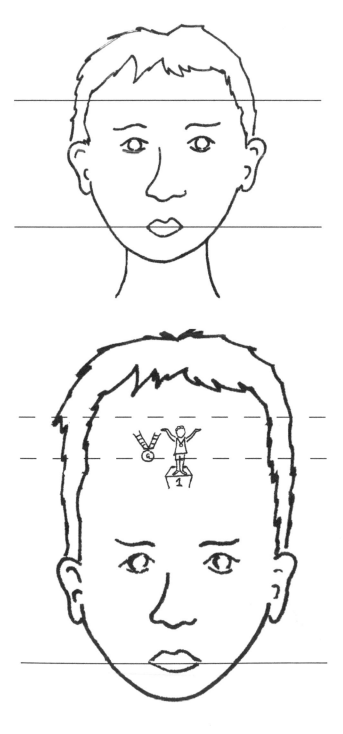

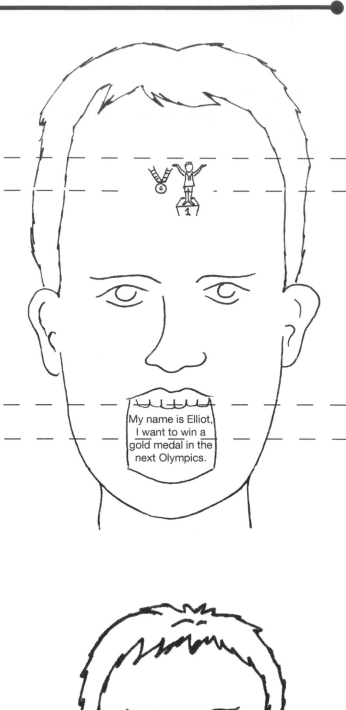

My name is Elliot, I want to win a gold medal in the next Olympics.

By lifting the top flap you can reveal his dreams and ambitions.

By pulling the bottom flap you can make him explain them.

© Giles Hughes and Brilliant Publications
Creative Homework Tasks, 7–9 Year Olds

Talking Heads

All About Me –
Self Portrait in a Box

The task for the children is to find objects and images that are imporrtant to them. Discuss with the children the task you have in mind. Talk over which items they might think to include to create their own personal self portrait.

For inspiration, look at modern artist, David Mach's *Portrait of the Nation*. The collage is made from magazine cuttings, books, posters, brochures and leaflets etc. It depicts Britain at work, rest and play and was commissioned for the Self Portrait Zone of the Millennium Dome at Greenwich. It is made on 15 separate panels and spans over 30 metres in length. For more information see **www.davidmach.com**.

The collage work of Peter Blake, famous for designing the Beatles Sgt. Peppers album cover, is also well worth investigating.

As well as creating stunning and interesting displays, this activity also gives the children opportunities to talk about themselves, their families, their hobbies and interests.

Draw up an A4 stencil like the one below, that you can photocopy. The children will use this sheet to make the tray for their self portrait. Give each child a copy.

A nice idea is to photocopy the boxes in different colours, then ask the children to find someone in their class with the same coloured box to talk with about the All About Me Box.

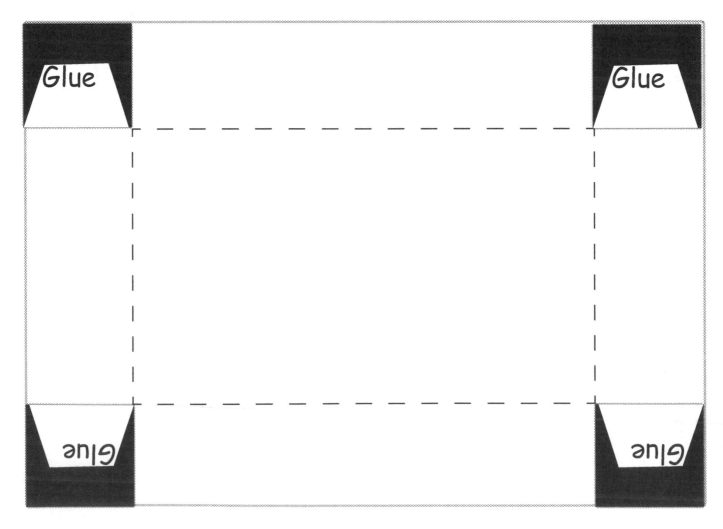

All About Me – Self Portrait in a Box

Your teacher will give you an A4 sheet of thick paper. Cut out the blackened areas, fold along the dotted lines and glue the tabs to the sides to construct an open tray.

In the tray you are going to create a unique self portrait made up of images and objects that are important to you.

Things that you might decide to include in your self portrait have been listed below.

Cut out, arrange and even colour the items that you have collected. Piece together your collage – it will represent the things that are important in your life. Glue them down.

When you get back to school, your teacher may ask you if you want to talk about your collage in circle time, explaining your choices.

Photographs of you as a baby and toddler

Photos of your family

Photos of your family pets or favourite animals

Photos of you enjoying a family holiday

Small toys

Favourite colours

Magazine cut-outs of your favourite pop stars, actors/actresses, comedians, sports heroes, etc

Scenes from your favourite film

Lyrics from your favourite song

Wrappers from your favourite sweets

Drawing Emotions

Challenge each child in your class to draw one of these emotions. You could then run a competition to see which pupil, or team of pupils, can match the correct emotions to each drawing.

Getting the children to explain their ideas and choices can be revealing!

Here is a list of 30 emotions:

Anger	Fear	Loneliness	Boredom	Frustration	Pain
Calmness	Grief	Nervousness	Courage	Happiness	Patience
Depression	Hate	Embarrassment	Disgust	Horror	Rage
Delight	Impatience	Sadness	Ecstasy	Joy	Shock
Elation	Kindness	Surprise	Peace	Love	Unhappiness

Drawing Emotions

What does anger look like? Sketch a picture of your ideas.

Think about what kind of lines to draw, slow and careful or quick and aggressive?

What colours might you choose to draw your picture? What colours do you think are angry colours?

Try drawing some other emotions, what do you think happiness and sadness look like?

Top Trumps!

The task for the children is to produce a 'Top Trumps' card about themselves, giving themselves a percentage score in each of the six categories and explain why they awarded each score.

Children love this activity, and if carried out responsibly, it can provide the catalyst for valuable debate at circle time, as well as raising children's self-esteem and self-confidence.

A nice way to start this activity is to tape a sheet of paper to everyone's back and ask the class to write a comment about what they like about this person or what they think is good about them. This informal opening is highly popular with most children and can lead to some interesting and revealing discussion during circle times.

Introduce each category to the class and list the kinds of skills, talents and qualities a person might need to score highly in that area.

This is a perfect time to talk about multiple intelligences and how different people learn and see things in different ways.

It is a good idea to encourage children to award themselves at least 90% in each category. The benefits of this are that the children who perceive themselves as under achievers are given a boost, while high flyers are still satisfied with a score of 99% or 100%.

When the Top Trumps Cards are returned to school, the class teacher can organize a 'whole class' game of Top Trumps.

Try reducing each card on the photocopier, so all children get their own set of class Top Trumps!

© Giles Hughes and Brilliant Publications
Creative Homework Tasks, 7–9 Year Olds

Top Trumps!

Your task is to produce a Top Trumps card about yourself. You will need to give yourself a percentage score for all the following categories:

Artistic ability – art, painting, drawing making things, music, drama

Citizenship – are you able to get on with classmates, teachers, dinner supervisors, etc? Are you good at making and keeping friends? Are you able to sort out other people's problems? Are you a school monitor or house captain?

Math magician – number work, mental maths, problem solving, data handling, shape and space

Language skills – writing stories, telling stories, listening to other people, making yourself understood, writing reports, speaking another language

Physical prowess – playing games, running, jumping, throwing, catching, swimming, balance, co-ordination, cycling

Science and technology – scientific knowledge, working things out, knowing about nature, fixing things, constructing models

Back at school your teacher will collect all the cards from your class. Now you can play 'My Class Top Trumps'.

How well do you know your friends and classmates? Play 'My Class Top Trumps' and find out!

John Smith
Artistic ability   97
Citizenship   95
Maths magician   100
Language skills   94
Physical prowess   98
Science /technology   92

Top Trumps!

Name

Top Trumps

Self Portrait

Artistic Ability

Citizenship

Maths Magician

Language Skills

Physical Prowess

Science and Technology

© Giles Hughes and Brilliant Publications
Creative Homework Tasks, 7–9 Year Olds

My Hero!

The task is for the children to create a pop-out hero card for a hero of their choice.

It is a good idea to have a class discussion about what makes someone a hero before setting this homework activity. Otherwise you tend to get a lot of footballers and soap stars. With a little input you can get your class to be more reflective and get a wider variety of responses. This can lead to some interesting topics for debate once the task is completed.

Follow the notes on the task sheet as a starting point for discussion and debate.

The completed pop-ups will fold flat (they can be kept in books or folders) or stand up for display.

My Hero!

What makes someone a hero?

- Is a fire fighter a hero when he charges into a burning building to save someone?

- Is a footballer a hero when he scores the winning goal in a cup final?

- Is a teacher a hero when she dedicates her time to help her pupils learn to read, write and know what it means to be a good person?

- Is a mother a hero when she has to work two jobs to support her children and still makes the time to show her children that she loves them?

What characteristics or qualities do heroes have?

Here are some ideas.

Loyalty
Selflessness
Courage
Perseverance
Determination
Dedication
Sacrifice
Bravery

Which qualities do you think are the most important?

 www.brilliantpublications.co.uk

© Giles Hughes and Brilliant Publications
Creative Homework Tasks, 7–9 Year Olds

My Hero!

Who is your hero?

Your task is to cut out and make this 'pop-out' hero card.

- *Carefully choose who your hero is and draw or glue on a picture of them.*

- *Find out as much as you can about them. Say why they are your hero.*

- *Say what qualities they have that make them so special.*

- *Say why you admire them.*

- *Has your hero inspired you to do something or live your life in a different way?*

Instructions

1. *Draw a portrait of your hero and write your information in the top square (you can use both sides).*

2. *Carefully cut out the pop-up template.*

3. *Score all dotted lines.*

4. *Carefully cut out the slit in the centre with a craft knife.*

5. *Fold top section forward and thread through the slit.*

6. *Fold bottom section up and glue tabs together.*

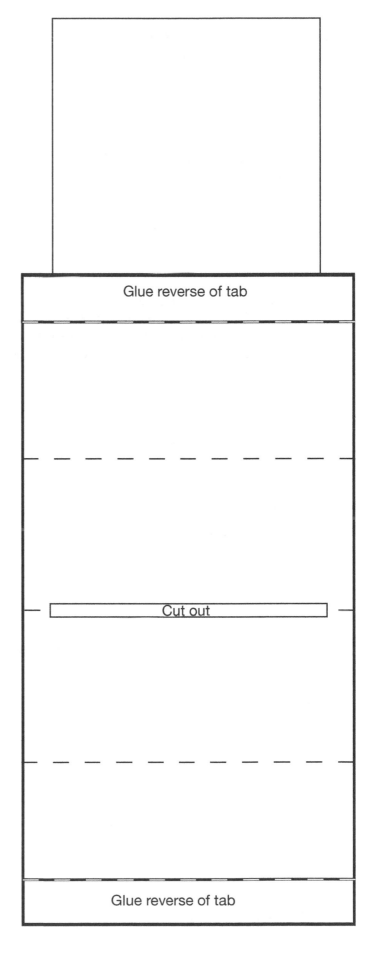

Glue reverse of tab

Cut out

Glue reverse of tab

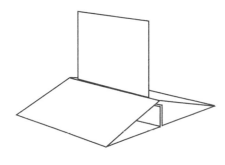

Living by the Rules!

The task for the children is to create a list of 10 new rules that every citizen or a new country must obey.

A nice introduction to this is to discuss the 10 commandments. Most children will be able to access this topic and no less than three world religions uphold them: Judaism, Christianity and Islam all believe that the 10 commandments were handed down by God himself and are therefore non-negotiable.

It can be fun to link some ideas the children will have to data found in surveys taken across the country. For example:

Don't kill

73% of Londoners came out most strongly against capital punishment.

Don't steal

20% of people in the West Country think it's OK to steal the office paperclips.

Respect your mum and dad

If you are a parent living in London or East Anglia, you are more likely to get grief from your kids than anywhere else in the UK – only 38% of children in these areas think respect for your parents is important!

Enjoy life

Only 32% of people in Tyne Tees thought enjoying life was important.

This list of rules can be used as a starting point or as an on-going evaluation of ideas:

Be honest

Don't kill

Look after the vulnerable

Respect your mother and father

Enjoy life

Nothing in excess

Be true to your own God

Treat others as you would like to be treated

Be true to yourself

Protect your family

Try your best at all times

Look after your health

Don't commit adultery

Live within your means

Appreciate what you have

Never be violent

Protect the environment

Protect and nurture children

Take responsibility for your own actions

Don't steal

Living by the Rules

Imagine that you have been elected Ruler of a new country!

Your first job is to come up with a list of 10 new rules that every citizen must obey – regardless of their gender, age, ethnicity or religion.

Your rules must be designed so that it makes the society your people live in safe and fair for all citizens.

Think carefully about your choices and how you word them.

Try not to repeat yourself – you might waste a rule!

Things to think about:
- Some things might seem obvious, like 'Don't kill people!' But can you think of another way of wording this so that all forms of violence are included   or do you think some violence is OK?

- There are some people who think that capital punishment is appropriate in some cases. What do you think?

- Think about the world we live in – what are the important issues today? How might your rules affect the environment, for example?

- Who are the most vulnerable members of society who need protecting the most? Most people agree that young children and old people are the most vulnerable. How might your rules help make their lives better?

- Which people in your life deserve respect? What does respect mean and how do you show it?

- Who do you look up to and admire? What qualities do they have? How could your rules promote these qualities?

For an extra challenge
Try writing your 10 rules in order of importance!